Awkward Moments

Awkward Moments
Celebrating the Humor in Life's Uncomfortable Situations

Specific House
One Wheatland St.
Burlington, MA 01803
781-272-9995
781-272-9996 (fax)

Printed in the United States of America

ISBN: 0-9674586-1-7

First Paperback printing: June 2001

Awkward Moments

CELEBRATING THE HUMOR IN LIFE'S UNCOMFORTABLE SITUATIONS

Laura & Wayne Gignac
Margie & Rick Segel

Specific House

Biographies

Wayne Gignac creates magic every time he presents *I Can't Wait to Go to Work*, his seminar on having fun at work. As a member of New England Speakers Association, Wayne, director of The Show Works, travels across the country, teaching the corporate world how to have fun at work. Wayne believes people, burdened by today's stresses, struggle to handle situations at work and at home. Being able to recognize stress, knowing how to deal with it, and allowing time to relax and enjoy life, is the lesson Wayne teaches his audiences. He gives steps to the way of changing hectic lives into fun, relaxing lifestyles. Wayne believes people are responsible for their own happiness and success.

Seven years ago, Wayne made a major move toward increasing his happiness, when he married Laura. An instant family was created as their marriage combined Wayne's two children and Laura's three children. They now are a family of seven! Laura, an early childhood/elementary school teacher, is home raising their five children: Justin, Amie, Dante, Marissa, and Joseph. At this time, Justin is attending the School of Visual Arts, in New York City. Amie is a sophomore in high school, and Dante is in eighth grade. Marissa is a sixth grader, and Joseph is a third grader. With a schedule which includes soccer, softball, band, and helping with school work, Laura happily looks forward to nine o'clock AM, when the house is empty and silent! During these off hours, Laura assists Wayne in the office.

While lying in bed, laughing about their crazy day, the concept of *Awkward Moments* came to life. Sharing these unexpected, uncomfortable moments with each other, helps bring Wayne and Laura closer. Through *Awkward Moments*, it is their intention to show others the common thread of vulnerability we all possess. And hopefully, then, we can all laugh (or cringe) together!

Margie and Rick Segel were childhood sweethearts from the time that they were 15 years old. They have been married for 32 years, and have worked together for the majority of that time. They owned one of New England's most successful woman's apparel stores for 25 years and currently operate Rick Segel & Associates, a speaking, training, and consulting firm specializing in "unzipping sales and marketing possibilities". They have three wonderful children who have supplied many of the awkward moments in this collection. Their children are now all married which allows Rick and Margie to travel throughout the world, speaking and gathering research for their programs and writings.

Rick is a Certified Speaking Professional (CSP) and has spoken over 1200 times on 3 continents. He is the past president of the New England Speakers Association, author of *Laugh and Get Rich, Romancing Your Customer*, and *Retail Business Kit for Dummies*. And Margie is always there to make sure all these things happen! A former elementary school teacher, Margie has blended her talents perfectly with Rick's to form a truly unique business. The exciting part of what they do is the exciting things that they do. Every day is different from speaking to bankers in Istanbul to bakers in Montana. Rick Segel & Associates provides business savvy in the most entertaining and positive approaches to continuing education.

AWKWARD MOMENTS

Justin Gignac--**book layout**--is also an artist & Advertising major at the School of Visual Arts in Manhattan. Born & raised in Norwich, Connecticut, Justin is the oldest child of five, in two families! Justin has held a number of eclectic jobs, from selling toys at FAO Schwarz to assisting in the running of a minor league basketball team. Although many would think his greatest accomplishment so far would be his 3 year stint as Tater the Gator, the mascot of the Double-A NY Yankees affiliate, we believe his lifetime stint as Wayne & Laura's oldest son is most special!

Raina Telgemeier--**Illustrator**--is an accomplished artist, born and raised in San Francisco, California who recently moved to New York City to study illustration at the School of Visual Arts. You might say that Raina is also an accomplished chef, specializing in microwave desserts. Her favorite dish is to melt her ice cream for a few seconds to obtain the perfect "mushy" consistency. *Awkward Moments* is Raina's first book, though we're sure it won't be her last.

Dedication

We want to thank our families and friends, who are a constant source of Awkward Moments. We look forward to celebrating many more Awkward Moments with them for years to come. Our newest Awkward Moment will be facing them after they read this book.

The Awkward Moments Gang

Awkward Moments

What is an awkward moment? It is that brief moment in time that we feel inept, embarrassed, unsure, or uneasy. It is when we feel dumb, stupid, or surprised. They are those brief seconds that seem like minutes and those minutes that seem like hours. It is the time we lose some of our self respect or self esteem or tarnish a little bit of our lofty self image. It is that humbling period of time when we lose our confidence and when the arrogant become mere mortals again.

We deal with this phenomenon with humor, laughter, frivolity, and self deprecating comments that make others laugh and make ourselves feel better. Laughter is the tool to cope with life's moments of awkwardness. Without laughter we wouldn't be able to cope or make it through the day or those trying moments. This book recognizes the awesome power of laughter and attempts to harness just a little of its power to help all of us laugh at ourselves as we see ourselves within these stories.

This book is about R E S P E C T. It is about respecting others and ourselves, and reminding us that life is made up of challenges and surprises. So join us in laughter, relate to us, or just enjoy life's *Awkward Moments.*

AWKWARD MOMENTS

Walking into the wrong public restroom

Leaving the bathroom stall, with an awful stench, to face others who are waiting their turn

When you notice that the dryer in the Ladies' Room is out of order. . . after you wash your hands

While flinging your hands around to "air dry", you step out of the bathroom, only to come face to face with your prospective client

When you take Xenical (a fat blocker diet medication), and you REALLY have to go to the bathroom

Using a bathroom with louver doors, and everyone in the next room can hear you

The Quicker Picker Upper

My wife and I were coming back from a vacation in New Hampshire with our three children: two daughters, three and five years old, and our six-month-old son. We were waiting to pay the cashier at the front of the restaurant. While waiting, my son, who was coming down with some type of stomach bug, proceeded to throw up on the floor in front of the cashier. It was a milky white substance that was so disgusting, I told the cashier I would clean it if she would give me a towel.

I crouched down on my hands and knees as the cashier handed me a filthy, dirty towel, which I used to start the cleanup. My wife, who was holding the baby, facing front, was watching me frantically work. Suddenly, our son proceeded to let loose one more time - this time on my head!

Shocked, I didn't know what to do! I didn't want to clean my head with this dirty towel, and the smell of this gunk was beginning to get to me. In desperation, I had my daughter take one of the napkin holders off the table, and I used about three hundred napkins to clean the floor and myself!

3

Should have checked the shoes

While solemnly announcing a tragedy during a live broadcast, a fly continually lands on the newscaster's face. Struggling to remain composed, he tries to shoo the persistent fly with repeated facial movements.

Eagerly revealing your intimate desire over the phone, only to learn you are on a speakerphone which is in a room full of people

Being picked from the audience to take part in a magic trick, up on stage

Keeping your eyes from glancing down, while talking to a lady with a low cut top

Knock First

While working under a deadline, a newscaster suddenly realizes the five cups of coffee are taking effect. Dropping everything, he rushes to the nearest bathroom, which is in the boss' office. Without knocking, he opens the restroom door to find his boss sitting on the toilet. Both men are too shocked to speak! Instantly, he turns and shuts the door, then realizes his suit coat is caught in the door. So, slowly, he opens the door again, apologizes, and slams the door shut.

Two For the Price of One

A friend recently passed away, and I went to the wake that was being held at a large funeral home. When I got there, I stood in line waiting to pay my respects. As I got to the body, I turned from the people I was speaking with and was shocked! There was a woman lying in the casket! My friend was a man! Had he been a cross dresser, or was I at the wrong wake? I was too embarrassed to say anything to the people around me, so I shook the hands of the immediate family and quietly left the room. There were actually two wakes taking place in this funeral home, and I had walked in on the wrong one! Thank God this was an inner awkward moment.

". . .And now, our Valedictorian."

AWKWARD MOMENTS

When you walk into a glass slider during a cocktail party

When you forget, after insisting you will remember

When you are visiting friends at their new address, and you walk into the wrong house

When you burp in mixed company

When you slip on ice, in front of a group of people

Stuck at the Pump

It's three o'clock in the afternoon, and you're car pooling the middle school soccer team to their game. Your tank is on empty, so you zoom into the next gas station. Cars are entering from the opposite direction, but you don't have time to maneuver around to go with the flow of traffic. So you pull up to the nearest available pump which quickly stops the approaching car. This causes a chain reaction, making the five other cars behind this one slam on their brakes. You pretend not to notice the chaos you've caused and jump out to pump your gas.

It's only when you're standing there, in plain view of the other six drivers, that you realize that your gas tank is on the opposite side of your car and the hose will not reach. Awkwardly, you smile to the driver facing you, return to your seat and back out of the space. Receiving dirty looks from the other five drivers as you pass, you drive around to the end of the line.

On the Thigh the Heart Lies

My friend, Martha, suffered from ovarian cysts that needed to be removed. Her gynecologist recommended a surgeon whom she felt was outstanding. Martha was alarmed, since she once knew a boy from grammar school with the same name. Sure enough! Little Howie Schligter was now an expert surgeon!

During her appointment, she and Howie briefly reminisced about their childhood days, then moved on to speak of the impending surgery. The date was set, but Martha left feeling uneasy about it all.

Finally, the day before her surgery, Martha devised a plan to offset her inevitable awkward situation by purchasing a package of temporary tattoos.

Imagine the shrill of laughter that next morning in the operating room, when the operating team discovered the artwork on her inner thigh, spelling out her undying love for "Little Howie" framed in a heart.

Asking a woman when the baby is due,
and finding out that she isn't pregnant!

The New Driver

It was hard to believe my parents so quickly trusted me with their Mercury Cougar. I got my license two weeks before, and already they were suggesting I pick up my younger brother from school. I wasn't sure about this, but not wanting to create any doubts in their minds, I agreed.

I wasn't worried about the driving, but I was concerned about driving around my brother's school. Xavier High has all guys, and is the brother school to my high school, Mercy High. Dismissal time at Xavier sends hundreds of guys out to the parking lot, all at once!

I wasn't sure I could drive with this much distraction. I arrived five minutes early so I could find a parking spot, out of the way of the buses, but with a great view! My brother had no problem finding me and jumped into the front seat.

"OK, let's go!" he said, feeling kind of cool, not to have Mom behind the wheel.

I spotted a few guys from the basketball team, who were checking out my car, so I smiled.

"OK, Laur, let's get out of here!" my brother urged.

"All right!" I answered, and shifted into drive. Stepping on the pedal, I prepared to move slowly ahead. But nothing happened! So I continued to press harder on the pedal, until it was on the floor. Panicked, I screamed to my brother there was something wrong! The car wouldn't move! My younger brother leaned over to me and laughed,

" Try stepping on the gas!"

Taking my foot off the brake, I started coasting out of the parking lot, hoping no one had noticed my panic attack.

Catching your coat in the revolving door

When your parents take you out for a fancy dinner, where they use finger bowls to clean between courses, and you think it's soup!

When you spit food at someone, while talking

When you're eating pizza, you take a bite and all of the cheese comes off

When you're eating pizza, and it burns the roof of your mouth

In the Big Leagues

My son was a ball boy for the Boston Celtics. My wife and I got tickets to see a nationally televised game; the Celtics verses the Chicago Bulls. I was so proud of my son - he was wearing his white satin Celtics uniform. I announced to complete strangers, who were sitting around us in the stands, HE was my son!

The game started and at 4:07, Michael Jordan fell. The referee called my son out to clean the court, since he specialized in cleaning sweat. Only this time, it wasn't sweat. Someone must have spilled something on the court before the game. The referee instructed my son to go to the locker room, for a hot, wet towel.

My son never hurries and this was no exception! He dawdled his way to the locker room, not realizing there were 14,000 people watching him, and countless more watching on TV. It seemed like an eternity before he returned with the towel.

Anxiously, my wife declared, "He doesn't clean his room. I'm going down there!"

Now, all the people near us were talking among themselves, saying, "That's HIS son!"

When my son finally returned and wiped the floor, Kevin McHale went over to him and whispered into his ear. As CBS took a close-up shot, he told my son that he had better get a good education, because he would make a lousy janitor!

Braces can be hazardous to your love life!

Which is Worse?

Giving a gift purchased at a real bargain, and forgetting to remove
the price tag

OR

Receiving a gift that still has the clearance price marked on the
price tag

Surprising a friend at home, and discovering her house is like a
war zone

OR

Overwhelmed by the disaster, and resigning yourself never to
entertain company, you open your door to find your friends from
work, surprising you with a visit!

Opening your hotel room door to find it occupied by a couple in a
very compromising position

OR

Settling into your hotel room with your spouse, only to be caught
by another hotel guest who is registered to the same room

Funny Looks

A blizzard was expected. It was mid-afternoon; I had several errands to run, and no car to use. Luckily, my sister and her husband agreed to drive me around before getting their kids from the school's early dismissal. While sitting in the back seat, mentally going over every errand, I absent-mindedly put Chapstick on my chapped lips.

Our first stop was to the photo shop. Handing in my slip, then paying for my order, I thought how strange this teenage girl was acting toward me. It was as though she thought I was mentally unstable! I didn't think too much of this, since we had a time limit and still so much to do. Next, we stopped at the post office, then the bank and finally the grocery store. My sister and her husband kept busy, listening to the closings and the updated weather reports, hardly taking notice of me entering or leaving the car. At each stop, I noticed people looking at me strangely.

After returning to the car from the grocery store, my sister turned to talk to me. She immediately screamed! My brother-in-law and I both jumped. She screamed again, this time in laughter, as she pointed to my face. Sitting up to the rear view mirror, I saw bright red lipstick smeared all over my mouth! It wasn't Chapstick© in my purse; it had been my tube of red lipstick! All the odd stares suddenly made sense to me! We all laughed hysterically, recounting all the stops we had made, and all the funny looks I had gotten everywhere.

Servers' Dilemma

Here it was! My first day flying solo as a server at THE most upscale restaurant in my shoreline resort community. Everything was going just as planned, when it happened. . . I tipped the vichyssoise and it spilled all over Mr. Pettibone, the president of the bank. Not only did I get soup all over him, but the china bowl crashed to the floor, causing everyone in the restaurant to look over and stare!

"No, I had the lobster bisque. It's my wife who ordered the vichyssoise," stated Mr. Pettibone, without skipping a beat. As laughter broke out through the room, I was thankful that Mr. Pettibone had diffused this entire awkward moment with a startling humorous comment.

Imagine this. . .You are working as a server in a four star restaurant and your customers have ordered an expensive bottle of wine. As everyone at the table is watching, you open the wine, trying to be as professional as possible. Suddenly, the cork pops from the bottle, and plunks right into a bowl of sauce, splashing everyone at the table!

Working Mom - OOPS!

Admitting you're lost after insisting you knew the way

Forgetting your place when you are telling a story

Being caught in a lie

Forgetting what you are saying

Being asked to respond, after you pretended to hear

Bigger Than It Looks

When I first got my GMC Suburban, I did not know where it would fit, and where it wouldn't fit. Unfortunately, the attendant at the car wash also had the same problem! He instructed me to pull my car in until my wheels caught the conveyor belt, and then to put my car into neutral.

Halfway through the carwash, while those big brushes were doing their thing on my car, and I couldn't see a thing outside, I realized that I had been in the same position for a long time. It hit me that I was stuck in the middle of a car wash! Other than blowing my horn, I didn't know what to do. Of course, the attendant didn't know what to do, either. So I ended up staying there for over an hour, until he got help. They yelled to me and I yelled to them. But what I repeatedly yelled was for them to shut off the water. Although I had horrible scratches on the roof of my truck, my truck had never been so clean. It was worth the awkward moment!

Famous Moments

President George Bush's vomiting at the Japanese Prime Minister's dinner

President Bill Clinton's facial expression when asked about the cigar, at the impeachment deposition

David Letterman's interview of a cursing, unruly Madonna

Baseball player Bill Buckner's through the legs play

Dan Quayle's misspelling of "POTATO"

Mistakenly calling your teacher, "MOM"

An acquaintance caringly asks, "So, how are you lately? You quickly blurt out that you have been suffering from a nasty cold and could hardly sleep last night, only to then realize that the question was meant for a mutual friend who is standing next to you.

Sharing an elevator with a couple who are deeply engrossed in an intimate conversation

Being introduced to a husband and wife, after you assumed they were father and daughter

Seeing someone who looks familiar - not being totally able to recall how you know them, yet they have intimate details about your relationship with them

First Date

While driving the car, with a beautiful woman, soft music playing, you break wind

A seemingly endless pause in the conversation

Eating, while sitting across from your date

Saying something totally stupid

The Highs and Lows of Blind Dates

The Facts of Life

When I explained the Facts of Life to my children, I used the book, *Where Do Babies Come From?* My children were very interested in this reading, but didn't ask any questions when we were all together. Later that evening, my son who was 6 years old, came up to me and asked me some very pointed questions.

"Did your penis get hard, Daddy?"

"Did you put your penis in Mommy?"

But most importantly, he asked me, "Did it feel good?"

My response was "Yes," and then my son walked away and never brought it up again.

Playing With the Big Kids

When I was a young boy, I used to love to play with the older boys in the neighborhood. They didn't always let me into their games, but on this one occasion I was finally included. However, after playing for a couple of hours, I had to go to the bathroom. I didn't want to spoil my fun and go home, so I went into the woods and relieved myself there. After using a leaf from a ground plant to wipe myself, I went back to play. Later that night my bottom got very sore. You see, I had used poison ivy to wipe myself! That was a very painful awkward moment.

Daddy! That's Disgusting!

We spent a beautiful day at the ocean side beach house, with a private beachfront, pool and Jacuzzi. Food and drink were plentiful and to be honest, I had a little too much to drink. Since I was not quite up to driving home, I sat near a window in the back seat with the kids for the return trip. The combination of the food, drink and car ride just didn't mix, but my wife was not able to pull over quickly enough for me to be sick at the side of the road. As I was vomiting out the window at 65 miles an hour, my kids yelled out, "Daddy! That's disgusting!"

Then, one of the kids pushed the automatic button for the car window, closing it on my neck! I began screaming for relief and absolution for my sins, while throwing up, because my air passage was being crushed. They finally released me, but not from the guilt I felt from my awkward moment. They couldn't tell me to stop drinking, because I was not that much of a drinker to begin with--the only comment from the kids was that I didn't smell good, and they would never drink when they grew up. Maybe my awkward moment had some value, after all.

Close Encounter

When traveling on a flight from Boston to Atlanta, I sat in front of a family of five: a mother, a father, and three loud, active children. They kept kicking the back of my seat and yelling in my ear. I glanced over a few times, with my best-disgusted look.

Halfway through the flight, I had to go to the bathroom. When I returned to my place, the father had his arms hanging over my seat. When I got closer, he asked me if I was associated with the company folder I had left on the seat.

I said, rather abruptly, "Yes, I am. I am the president of the company!"

He said that it was such an honor to meet me! I was puzzled until he told me that he had just signed a major contract with my firm. Who could have guessed? During the rest of the flight, I didn't mind those kids at all. Boy, was I glad I never really said anything to him about the kids!

Which is Worse?

Spotting someone picking their nose

OR

Being spotted, while picking your nose!

_____

Forgetting what you went upstairs to get

OR

Returning downstairs because you've given up on trying to remember, then remembering

Onion Breath

AWKWARD MOMENTS

You're picking up your suitcases after a crowded flight, and your bag is one of the first ones to come out on the conveyer belt. As you pick it up, the suitcase opens and your dirty underwear falls out and goes around on the belt.

Seat belt extenders - those extra few inches that the flight attendant distributes to larger passengers

Being so large that you become stuck in the aisle of the airplane

When you're on a plane and you and another passenger have the same seat number. You complain to the flight attendant, and find out you have boarded the wrong plane.

Leaving My Mark

During my freshman year at college, I was invited to Houston, Texas for Thanksgiving. My friend told me to bring a suit because it was debutante season and I would be going to various parties. At this one particular outdoor party, which I attended with a lovely Southern lady named Lee Flowers, the temperature in Houston was in the nineties, and the humidity was oppressive. This was very different for me since I was from Boston, where it was always cool, or even cold, at Thanksgiving time.

The only suit I owned was a heavy, wool, 3-piece herringbone suit, which certainly was not appropriate for this affair. But, I had no options. I was able to position myself under the shade of a tree, where we sat on a newly shellacked redwood bench. After sitting for about an hour, I went to get up and realized that my pants were stuck to the red wood bench! I frankly did not know what to do.

I cleared my throat as I forced my pants off the bench and worried that I would have a huge hole in them. As I casually felt my backside, trying hard not to be too conspicuous to my date, I was relieved to find no holes in my pants. But as I glanced back to the redwood bench, I saw the impression of herringbone wool, outlining my derriere. The most awkward part was when I watched the reaction of my hosts, knowing that I was the only one who could have possibly left that mark.

Newly divorced, and your girlfriend's husband hits on you

When you've changed your last name due to a remarriage, and then have to explain your relationship to your child to every new teacher, coach, scout leader, PTA member, etc.

Going out with a good friend who is in the midst of a divorce and talks only about the divorce

When you call your husband by your ex-husband's name

"EXCUSE ME!"

"Can I play, too?"

Traveling Guide Dog

A blind man, with his guide dog, is flying cross-country. While sitting on the plane at a stopover, the pilot comes back to see the dog and visit a bit with this passenger. Hearing that the dog has been traveling for seven hours without an opportunity to relieve himself, the pilot immediately offers to take the dog outside for a walk. The passenger is thankful for the help, and sends the dog off with the pilot.

Being familiar with this airport, the pilot takes the dog out to a place away from the traffic. After a short while, the pilot realizes the only way to return to the plane is through the terminal. With his sunglasses still on, the smiling pilot passes through the crowd of passengers waiting to board his flight. The looks of shock and horror surprise him, until he realizes that it's because he is in his pilot uniform, wearing dark glasses and holding onto the harness of a guide dog!

Forgetting your loved one's birthday

Being asked by your wife, "Does this make me look fat?"

Nearly forgetting your wedding anniversary, you come home with a straggly bunch of flowers from the supermarket

Trying to have an adult conversation with a friend as persistent children hang around

Sending out extra wedding invitations expecting that some people won't come, and they ALL show up

Cutting in Line

It's three o'clock in the afternoon, and you're car pooling the middle school soccer team to their game. Your tank is on empty, so you zoom into the next gas station. Cars are entering from the opposite direction, but you don't have time to maneuver around to go with the flow of traffic. So you pull up to the nearest available pump which quickly stops the approaching car. This causes a chain reaction, making the five other cars behind this one slam on their brakes. You pretend not to notice the chaos you've caused and jump out to pump your gas.

It's only when you're standing there, in plain view of the other six drivers that you realize that your gas tank is on the opposite side of your car and the hose will not reach. Awkwardly, you smile to the driver facing you, return to your seat and back out of the space. Receiving dirty looks from the other five drivers as you pass, you drive around to the end of the line.

While making love with spouse, your three-year-old calls out, "Mommy, is that you?"

Being evicted from your apartment because of neighbor complaints that your bed squeaks too much at night

The one morning you decide not to make the bed and straighten up the house, your in-laws decide to surprise you with a visit

While making love, your eight-year-old appears on the scene

Losing Mother

I was on a recent business trip to Cedar Rapids, Iowa. I had flown there from Minneapolis and when I went to baggage claim, my bags didn't appear. There was a nice, young, married couple who appeared to be having the same problem. We looked at each other and agreed we should report it to the airline agent.

Arriving at the counter, the agent said, " I know, you're looking for your bags. They didn't make this flight, but they are coming in on the next one. We will deliver them to you."

It seemed fair enough to me, but the young lady started to freak out. "I'm not leaving without my mother!" she screamed.

The agent and I looked at each other. We couldn't imagine what she was talking about! I then looked at the lady's husband, because he was trying to calm her down. The lady hit her husband and yelled at him for packing the urn in the suitcase.

"I told you we should have put her in the carry-on luggage!" she cried.

Yes, you've got it. Her mother had just died, was cremated, and the urn was in the suitcase. Talk about an awkward moment. What could you say?

46

Pretending to like some food that you absolutely hate, and then being offered seconds

When your daughter-in-law catches you sitting on the toilet because you left the door open

When your parents invite your future in-laws to dinner, and Dad falls asleep at the head of the table

Trying to spare someone's feelings after receiving an ugly gift

What Time Is It?

Fred is one of the nicest and sweetest men I know. Fred holds a Ph.D. in physics but, unfortunately, has a degenerative eye disease and is nearly blind. His eyes have gotten so bad that it has forced him to use a white cane. Fred has become the real life "Mr. Magoo". His sight is not about to slow him down.

We both attended a Professional Speakers Conference where we ended up at the same break out session. Just as I arrived, I noticed the speaker ask Fred if he would help pass out the handouts. The speaker even walked right over the cane to give Fred the handouts. Fred certainly wasn't going to say that he couldn't manage this task and so he proceeded to pass out the handouts as best he could. He was OK with that because people were calling out for the handouts and Fred responded to the sounds of their voices. But then the speaker announced that if anyone needed a handout, they should just raise their hand.

Fred was in trouble! I knew he would never admit defeat, so I yelled to him, "Fred, it's Rick. I'm in the back, I'll help you."

I then said 9:00 o'clock indicating where a hand was up. Then 6:00 o'clock. Then 11:00 o'clock. Each time Fred knew where the person was who needed the handout. It worked and Fred and the speaker were saved from a very awkward moment.

What Does It Look Like?

Sometimes I wish I could just follow Fred around, because he is an endless source of material. Just a couple of months ago, Fred and I took a flight together. Fred was able to get a seat up front and I was back in row twenty-five or thirty. I told Fred to wait for me, since I was going to be driving him home.

Did Fred wait? No way! He rushed down to claim his luggage. When I finally caught up with him, he was already at baggage claim, searching for his bag. If you have seen a blind person look for a bag, then you will understand, but for those of us who haven't, it is a unique experience because it is done by touch. Fred was feeling every bag to find his. I realized that this was a very difficult task to perform, so I offered to help.

Then, I asked the stupidest question of my life, "Fred, what does it look like?"

Fred turned to me and said, laughingly, "I don't know. I'm blind!"

AWKWARD MOMENTS

When you smash up your girl friend's father's car

When you are kissing your date good night to the whistling sounds of your nose

When you rush into school with wet feet and meet slippery tiles

When your seventeen-year-old son comes home after drinking, runs upstairs and throws up - while you have two tables of bridge downstairs and can hear everything

"Oh No! I thought I pushed the button!"

The Rest of the Story. . .

Our illustration shows how awkward driving through a garage door might be, but now, as Paul Harvey says, "The Rest of The Story".

My mother was never very mechanical, but she loved the remote control garage door opener. She thought it was the best. She loved driving right into the house, as she would say.

The problem was she did everything very quickly. So the morning she drove into the garage door, she had pushed her remote control and just assumed it would work. Without looking, she proceeded to back up. But the door hadn't gone up! Noticing this, she hit the button again. But at the exact same time, she depressed the gas pedal and smashed into the garage door, which had just started to rise.

With the car through the door, both the garage door and the car went up. As my mother and the car were being lifted, she had the good sense to hit the remote control again. This time it stopped, holding the car with its back tires off the ground. Her house looked like the front of a Hard Rock Café. Talk about awkward! She couldn't face the neighbors for weeks.

AWKWARD MOMENTS

When you've stepped in your dog's doo doo, and then track through your neighbor's house

When your dog craps in dog obedience class

When a dog starts "humping" your leg

When your dog jumps up on your company with muddy paws

When you bring your dog to a neighbor's house and it wets on the rug

Marines to the Rescue

When my daughter Lori was fourteen years old, we decided we would send her to a theme camp for a summer camp vacation. Since she loved skiing, this seemed like a natural choice. After researching the possibilities, we found a ski camp for children aged fourteen to seventeen, guided by a professional skier from New York. He and an assistant would take the kids to Chile, where they would work on their racing skills for a three-week session. After checking references and talking to kids who had gone in previous years, we felt we had made a good choice.

We met the instructor and the other children and parents at the airport. Although we were still nervous about letting her go so far away, we felt confident we had chosen an interesting, yet safe and protected camping experience. We told Lori to call us as soon as she got to Chile to let us know everything was fine.

But we didn't hear from her that day, or the following, or the following. We even tried calling the contact number we had been given, but the person who answered the phone did not speak English and just hung up on us. At this point, we were getting very concerned and started to contact the other parents. They had not heard from their kids either, so we formed a hotline to update each other upon contact from our kids.

On the fourth day, we still hadn't heard from her and I decided to get to the bottom of the matter. I contacted the Chilean consulate in Boston, explained the situation, and was told to call back at 4:00 PM for more information. When I called back at 4:00 PM, I was told that I would hear from my daughter at 7:00 PM that same day. He did tell me the kids were safe and everything was fine.

At exactly 7:00 PM, the phone rang. It was my daughter, crying, "Daddy, what did you do? Marine helicopters landed on the mountain looking for us. The marines told the director of the camp to make sure that all of the kids called home and they especially asked for me! I'm so embarrassed! No other parents sent the marines to find their kids!"

That might have been an awkward moment for her, but it was a major relief for me to know that Lori was safely skiing in Chile, and having a wonderful time.

"Would you guys keep it down!
I'm trying to do a funeral!"

While having sex with your spouse, your dog sneaks up from behind, to sniff your butt

While having coffee and cake with friends, your dog jumps up to the table and snatches a piece of cake from a plate

Strangely, your dog lies next to your guest and licks her shoe. After sharing an awkward laugh over this, the guest stands to move away, only to slip and fall due to the wet shoes.

When your dog steals the roast beef cooling on the kitchen counter, just as the dinner guests arrive at the front door

AWKWARD MOMENTS

While your mouth is stretched open in angles you didn't think possible, your dentist asks, "So, how's the family?"

When you have to bring a sample of your fresh sperm to have it examined after a vasectomy, but your appointment is at 3:00PM and you must leave from work. Where do you go to collect this sample? Wherever you go - it's an awkward moment!

Sitting in the examining room with nothing on but a johnny - waiting, and waiting, and waiting

60

Hello Meter

At our vacation home, we were waiting for the tree surgeon to arrive to let us know how much it would cost to remove some of the enormous pine trees we had in our yard. When the unmarked pick-up truck pulled up to the driveway, I quickly went out and introduced myself and asked the man what his name was.

He said, "Meter Reader."

I responded, "Hello, Meter."

Suddenly, I realized he was not the tree surgeon, but the man who reads the electric meter for the house. I felt so stupid when he repeated, loudly and distinctly, "I AM THE METER READER!"

This borders on a stupid moment, as well as an awkward one.

Read It and Weep

A CEO of a large company, going through a divorce, offered his wife a settlement that he thought acceptable. However, on the day of the proceedings, his company was in the news since it was being bought out in a hostile takeover. The value of his company, as broadcasted in the news, was significantly higher than the amount the husband was claiming it to be. Imagine the husband's reaction when the wife's attorney brought in the business section of the newspaper!

Stumped

With the popularity of SUVs, there are a lot of people driving them who have no right to be behind the wheel of a vehicle with that much power. I am one of those people.

The most awkward moment I ever had was when I decided to go "4-wheel driving" in my back yard, over a tree stump. Unfortunately, I somehow got the stump wedged between the right front tire and the body of the vehicle. Although these trucks are supposed to drive through everything, I got stuck in my own back yard!

The embarrassment was beyond belief, when I had to call a tow truck to tow my 4-wheel drive, all terrain vehicle from my own backyard. My friends and family have never let me live down that awkward moment!

Getting Trapped in Conversation

The moment after your drooling pet St. Bernard shakes his head, while in a crowd

Your dog begins to sniff a passerby, only to be greeted with an awful scent, which sends the dog away, whimpering.

Whenever your cat uses your mother's leg as a cat post

While visiting at your friend's home, your dog tears apart a cherished cushion

They Are Still Here!

I had some important papers that I needed my mother to sign. Since my mother was not a technology whiz, I set it up at the local copy shop for her to receive the fax there, sign the papers, and then fax them back to me. Everything was going as planned, she received the fax, signed the form, and then sent it back to me. Then she called me, in a panic.

She screamed into the phone, "You'll never get the papers back!"

I asked why, in astonishment, and she answered, "Because they are still here!"

The Hat Stretcher

My mother was a milliner, and the challenge she always faced was getting the correct hat size for the customer. The easiest way to do this was to simply put the hat on a hat stretcher. But many times, a good milliner could stretch it just enough by pulling the hat with her hands, eliminating the need for the hat stretcher. On this one particular time, when she tried to do such a procedure for a customer who really wanted to buy the hat, the hat ripped into two pieces.

As the customer said, "I don't want it, now."

My mother replied, "Of course not."

"Mom, her breasts don't look fake to me!"

A nursing mother's leaking breasts

Asking an expectant mother if she is having twins, and she isn't

Seeing a new baby and saying, "What a cute boy" when it's a little girl

Asking someone why they look so bad, and they are really feeling fine

Telling someone that their weight loss looks great, and then remembering you heard something about them having a serious illness

Joy to the World

During a crowded Christmas Eve service, our four-year-old, busying himself, got his finger caught in a hole in the metal framework of the kneeler. My wife, who first noticed our trapped son, bent down to free him. Finding that the finger was quickly swelling and our son's patience was running out, she tugged on my arm, pulling me over to the dilemma. My father noticed the hushed commotion and bent down, too.

His little finger was red and puffy, so I stopped twisting it and decided to apply my saliva. Unfortunately, in panic situations such as this, my mouth becomes bone dry! So I asked our son to spit in my hand. Immediately, my wife and father began to gather their spit.

Afraid this escapade would bring the service to a halt in order to rescue the finger, I began to examine how the kneeler was made, and wondered how quickly we could detach it from the pew.

Just as the congregation raised their voices in song, our four-year-old began to cry, afraid that he was trapped forever. A woman in the pew behind us watched the four of us down on the floor, and realized the problem. She gave us her hand lotion, which we quickly lathered on his finger. As if on cue, his swollen finger popped out of the hole as the choir sang, "Joy to the World". Awkward as it was, we gave thanks that Christmas for a little bit of lotion.

Criticizing a coworker, not realizing
he's listening.

AWKWARD MOMENTS

Walking in on someone getting undressed

Accidentally scratching someone and drawing blood

Leaving your size tag out of your sweater, and it is a double extra large

Tripping on your hem

Wearing a uniform skirt on a windy school day

Trying to Act Cool

It was an awesome June day! The sun was hot, school was out, and my summer job wouldn't start until next week. Time to go cruisin'! I picked up Eric and we headed for the mall. We had no money for shopping, but we heard a lot of girls talking about shopping for bathing suits and stuff. We'd cruise the parking lot to see if it was worth our time to go inside.

We had circled around a couple of times when Eric spotted three girls on the sidewalk. One of the girls had been in my science lab and she was totally hot! Slouching a bit behind the wheel, I pulled up next to them. Eric called out, asking if they'd like some company! In my shock, I stared at Eric and totally forgot to watch the road.

BAM! WHOA! I thought my car was going to flip! Two tires were up on the sidewalk and we were headed for a fire hydrant! The girls screamed and Eric swore at me. Slamming on the brake, I tried to return to the road, like this was no big deal! We could hear the girls' laughter as I pulled away. Eric was totally bummed and called me all kinds of names. I decided to stick to the open road and carefully headed to the exit.

"And this is uh, . . .uh, . . .uh. . ."

Offering to treat before finding you left your money in your other pants

Insisting on treating, then having your credit card rejected

Offering to treat before finding you don't have enough money

Repeating the same point, on the same page

Those Nuts Look So Real!

It was a mid-October day and the downtown store window was decorated with synthetic autumn leaves and plastic acorns. We knew that the window display was a success when the following experience took place:

A salesperson was waiting on a customer at the front rack, which backed the window display. With the customer's back to the rack, the salesperson, who was facing the window, saw a live squirrel with the plastic acorns in its mouth scurry across the partition, twitching its tail, causing dust to fly everywhere. The salesperson, observing what was going on, did not want to alarm the customer, since the salesperson worked on commission and was in the middle of a really good sale. If she startled the customer, the sale would go out the window! Her awkward moment was remaining calm while keeping tabs on both her customer and the squirrel, making sure the two never met.

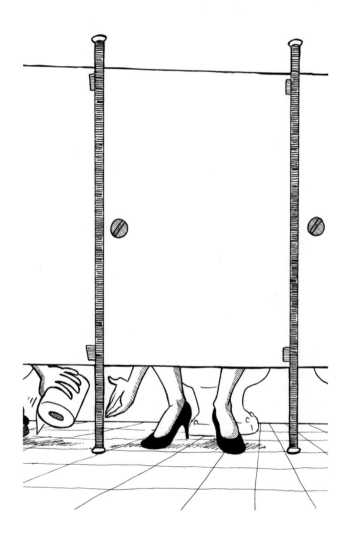

Calling everyone's attention to tell a hilarious joke, then forgetting how to tell it

Finding a situation funny when no one else does

Telling a joke and no one laughs

Uncontrollable laughter during a funeral

Realizing after you've begun to tell a joke that this joke really is inappropriate, and shouldn't be told

Uncle Pat

My uncle, Pat Taylor, was born and raised in County Cork, Ireland and had moved to the States when he was a teenager. He had brought with him a love of life with the friendliest twinkle in his eye. He passed away, but the rabbi (yes, Uncle Pat was one of the few Jews from Ireland) who was doing the eulogy, didn't know my uncle personally since Pat was not a very religious man. He had interviewed the family prior to the funeral to customize his remarks, but somehow must have misunderstood how my uncle was described. At the graveside service, he told the mourners that Pat was "a fun loving man who loved to play the piano".

My aunt, who was as fun loving as her husband, and loud and outspoken, blurted out, "Who the hell is he talking about? Pat never played the piano-he just loved to stand around it, drinking and singing."

When the mourners heard this outburst, they didn't know if they should be laughing or crying, and many did both.

Which is Worse?

Sitting in a chair at a friend's house, causing it to break

OR

A friend sits down in your chair, which breaks,

leaving her on the floor

Repeating gossip about an unnamed coworker, only to learn you

are speaking to the unnamed coworker

OR

Eagerly listening as someone shares a bit of gossip about some

unnamed coworker, and realizing they're talking about you!

Stopping Short

"How many sexual partners have you had?"

The Divorced Dad

In 1991, my 11-year-old son, Justin, had a science fair project on HIV. I suggested we go to the local hospital for pertinent information. As a divorced dad, eager to help, I arranged to have my son watch an actual HIV screening.

The nurse was very thorough with the information, and my son was writing fast and furiously. I was feeling pretty proud of myself for having set up this exceptional educational experience for Justin. Just then, the nurse asked if I was ready for the blood work, and asked if we should conduct the HIV screening as she does with all her clients. Certainly, I announced, not wanting Justin to miss a thing. Justin smiled at me and nodded. Quickly, I unbuttoned my cuff and began to roll up my sleeve. Not being a big fan of needles, I was focusing on being nonchalant in front of my son.

The nurse said, " Oh, before we draw your blood, I have several questions about your sexual history. How many sexual partners have you had?"

Suddenly, it occurred to me that Justin **must** have collected plenty of information on HIV, and hopefully was beginning to incur writer's cramp! To this day, I'm not sure who felt more awkward.

AWKWARD MOMENTS

When you pay to attend a New Year's Eve celebration, then realize you're the only people over the age of 50! You feel like you're at a high school prom!

When you are playing softball in an 'over 40' league and a fly ball comes to you, hits you on the head, and knocks you out

When you are skiing and you fall down under the chair lift while everyone is watching you

When you return a wave, which was really directed to the person behind you

The Big Spill

One Christmas Eve, my family of five was traveling to Maine for a week of skiing. Prior to the journey, we had stopped at our neighbors for some "Christmas Cheer". In my efforts not to drink before a long drive, I took a beer and nursed it along. All of a sudden, one of the kids bumped my elbow, which caused the beer to spill on my sweater. Since we were already packed, we left with me wearing this stained and smelly sweater.

It was a snowy, icy night, and there weren't many cars on the road. Because of the nasty winter weather, it was difficult to drive without swaying in my lane. All of a sudden, I saw a State Trooper following me with his lights flashing and I realized he wanted me to pull over. He came up to the car and asked for my license and registration. I saw him grimace when he caught a whiff of my beer soaked sweater.

At that point, he asked me to get out of the car and walk a straight line. He had assumed that the swaying was due to a little too much to drink. When I returned back to the car, my daughter announced from the back seat, "Officer, my daddy wasn't drinking--he always drives like that!"

I didn't know what way the trooper would take it, but he smiled and told me to continue our journey. Thankfully I avoided an expensive awkward moment.

"BAM!"

When you overshoot the tollbooth, and have to get out of the car to pay the toll

When your car gets stuck in the car wash

When you forget where you parked your car

When you drive up to an ATM machine, only to have over shot the machine. So you put your car in reverse and dart back, to the crunch sound of the car behind you.

The Unexpected Welcome

Becky and I were scheduled to return from our honeymoon Sunday night. We had a large, traditional wedding, and our trip to Bermuda was exactly what we needed.

We had planned to spend Sunday shopping in Boston after landing at Logan Airport. But once we were there, we decided to go home. Going home early would give us a chance to unpack and relax before visiting our families.

It was great coming home to our new apartment. After starting the laundry and checking our mail, which my mom had dropped off while we were gone, Becky suggested we break in our new mattress!

As we lay in bed after making love, we heard the telephone ring downstairs. I suggested that I give Becky a piggyback ride to the phone, in memory of all the moped rides we had shared. Excitedly, she hopped off the bed onto my back. When we got to the living room doorway, suddenly we heard "Surprise!"

Our entire families, including a few aunts and uncles and grandparents, were standing there. Becky and I were frozen in a state of shock for what seemed to be forever. After that, my mom returned her key to our apartment and has vowed to call before visiting!

SURPRISE!!!

Waking up from sleepwalking, while sleeping at a friend's house

Being caught daydreaming during class

Wetting the bed during a Boy Scout sleep over

Peeing at your desk in first grade, because the teacher wouldn't call on you to let you go to the bathroom

Catching your son, who is sleepwalking, opening the hamper and peeing into it

Polly Want A Cracker?

We took our three children on a vacation to St. Kitts in the Caribbean. On the way to the dining area, we passed the bar with a huge parrot in a cage. My ten-year-old daughter, who was sweet and innocent, ran to the parrot and said, "Polly want a cracker?"

The parrot looked at her and said, "Screw You!"

My poor daughter started to cry and thought that the parrot didn't like her. We found out later that the parrot only knew that one phrase. My daughter has never talked to a parrot again!

Tennis Anyone?

When my kids were little, my wife and I got tickets to go to the Volvo Tennis Tournament semi-finals in North Conway, NH. I don't remember who Jimmy Connors was playing, but he was about ready to serve when the public address announcer interrupted the game by calling out my name. He stated that I had an emergency phone call.

I quickly made my way through the stands to the closest telephone, only to find out that my three-year-old daughter had stuffed Play Doh up her nose and the babysitter didn't know how to get it out.

"Uh-Oh!"

When your child asks, in front of his friend and parent, "Can Johnny come with us to the circus? Please!!"

When you are attending the library's story time with your child, who is trying out "big boy underpants", and he stands up, pulls his pants down, and pees

When a little boy's penis gets stuck in the teeth of the zipper

While out in your yard, talking with a new neighbor, your little child announces that he has to go to the bathroom. You absently tell him to go on then, and go to the bathroom. He immediately drops his pants and pees.

The Doctor Without Patience

When playing softball, I somehow hit myself in the leg with the baseball bat and caused a large swollen area. All of my teammates thought that I should have it looked at in the hospital. As the doctor examined me, he ordered an ultrasound exam. While I was being examined with the ultrasound, the technician was concerned about a blood clot and called in an intern. He was also very concerned about a specific area. So they called in the head of the department.

This woman was a small, tough lady on a mission. She proceeded to examine my leg, but yelled at the intern and the technician for not having me lie flat on my stomach. Then she ran the ultrasound equipment over my leg. After a couple of passes, she proclaimed that there was nothing wrong with my leg, and that the duo had wasted my time and hers. At that point, I tried to interrupt, but she wouldn't let me speak, continuing to reprimand the two individuals. When I finally couldn't take it any longer, I yelled out to the head doctor, "Shut UP!!"

This was very bold and disrespectful in retrospect, but I had to stop her. As annoyed as a doctor could be with a patient, she said "WHAT?"

I responded quietly, "Doctor, you are examining the wrong leg!"

When you forget your boss' name, while you are introducing him

When you've buttoned your shirt wrong and don't notice it until a coworker points it out

When your boss' son is on your little league team

When you get spaghetti sauce on your shirt at a business lunch

When you are at a cocktail party, with serious business networking, and you find your fly is down

"I think you need a tissue."

See No Evil

My friend, an optometrist for some ten years, received a call from a mother about her eight-year-old son. Although the optometrist had built his practice to accommodate senior citizens, he agreed to see the boy. After giving this boy a serious mini lecture on the importance of being accurate and the seriousness of this kind of examination he proceeded with the exam.

With one eye covered, he began changing the lens, asking repeatedly, "Which is better, this or this?"

Finishing the exam of the first eye, he moved onto the second eye. This is where the trouble began.

"Which is better, this or this?"

"I, uh. I, uh", the boy answered.

"Well, which is better? Is it this one or this one?"

"Uh, I can't see!" he quietly said.

As the mother began scolding her son for fooling around, my friend noticed that he had flipped the wrong lens down and the boy truly couldn't see!

The optometrist quickly changed lenses trying to maintain his professionalism, realizing how ridiculous he appeared to this boy and his mom!

As an older gentleman enters the daycare, you ask which child is his grandchild. He replies, "None! Emily is my two year old daughter!"

While talking with another mother of a young child, at your nephew's christening, your zealous three-year old grabs a cookie away from her child and begins to eat it.

Holding your infant up to your shoulder, he silently spits up, which runs down your back. Having no clue of this, you're wondering why people behind you are noisily moaning in disgust.

Totally caught off guard, your infant vomits her lunch on the floor at the mall. As you frantically search for something to use to clean up this mess, an unsuspecting shopper slips and falls in it!

Kid on the Loose!

A Dressy Affair

After a long wait, I was sent to the examining room, told to take off all of my clothes, leave my shoes on, and put on a hospital johnny. After putting on the johnny (which didn't fit), I sat on the examining table. If someone is going to leave me alone in a room for forty-five minutes, I am going through the drawers. There was so much to look at in the room. I started playing with all of the diagnostic tools that were there: the blood pressure cuff, the stethoscope, and the flashlight.

Then I found the latex gloves. I had just put these on when the doctor walked in. She looked at me wearing the gloves, a hospital johnny that didn't fit, and my black shoes, and said in a firm voice, "Why are you wearing latex gloves?"

I had to think quickly. My response was, " Well Doc, I knew you were going to be wearing gloves, and I thought this was a dressy affair."

To this day, I don't know if she got it, but it sure was an awkward moment.

Which is Worse?

Repeatedly calling a supervisor by the wrong name,
then being told about it later from someone else

OR

Hearing your employee repeatedly call you by the wrong name.
The first few times, you think he misspoke, then you realize that he
has no clue what your name is!

Helping Mom do the laundry, and finding her thong panties

OR

Doing the laundry with your ten-year-old daughter, when she
uncovers your thong!

Excitedly tell a story, only to be interrupted midway, by the listener,
who reminds you you've already told the story, five times

OR

Talking with a friend, who excitedly bursts into telling you a story
she has told you about five times: do you listen again, and fake your
amusement, or interrupt with the punch line?

Life's A Beach

Deb, Vicki and I were psyched to spend the summer on the beach. While lying there, dozing, I thought I felt a slight tickle move across my shoulder. I carelessly ran my hand across my collarbone, in an effort to brush it away.

Thinking I must have imagined the tickle, I continued to doze. Suddenly, the tickle turned to a prick! I quickly reached up to my chest and felt something hard wiggling.

I hate crawling things and this was on me!! As I jumped up, it fell down into my bathing suit. Reaching in and trying to retrieve it only pulled the suit away from me, allowing the intruder to fall deeper! AAAHHHH!!!

I began dancing about my blanket, screaming, "It's getting me. AAAHHHH!"

Whatever it was, it was pinching my skin everywhere it went. Finally, I yanked down my bathing suit top and stood there stunned to see a little crab scurry off my blanket into the sand. I had little red marks where it had left its trail down to my stomach. Relieved that the crab was gone, I froze as I realized everyone was staring at me as I stood there, totally topless!

The Talking Computer

When I was the news director of a medium market radio station, I experienced one of my most memorable awkward moments. This was in the days when AM Radio was still king and FM was relatively new. Our FM, like many others at that time, was automated. The problem was the equipment used to automate it had been pieced together over the years from equipment abandoned by other, smarter radio stations. It was under the constant care of our chief engineer, Alex.

It was Saturday, Alex was out of town, and FRED, our nickname for this room-sized monstrosity, was acting up. About twice every hour the computer would lock up and I would be beckoned to take care of the problem by a series of ear piercing alarms. I was preparing our six o'clock news report when FRED yelled for me again. I had had it. I raced down the stairs screaming expletives back at FRED. When I got downstairs, I continued my tirade, screaming at Fred, using words that would make Popeye blush. Finally I got FRED back on track.

It wasn't until I started walking back upstairs that I noticed Sister Marie sitting quietly outside the door. I think she was hoping I wouldn't see her. But too late. We were both trapped. I sheepishly said hi and began to apologize when she quickly handed me the Public Service Announcement for the upcoming church bazaar, said that she could see I was busy, thanked me and left me standing there, wondering how I would ever face her again.

Coming back down the aisle from Communion, only to realize your coat hanger is attached to your coat's belt

While singing aloud one of your favorite melodies in Church, you joyfully start verse three, while everyone else concludes verse two

While praying aloud, in unison with the congregation, you continue on, even though everyone else has paused

At a funeral, when the priest leaves his microphone on during a bathroom break, and the congregation hears the sound of the flow, hitting the water

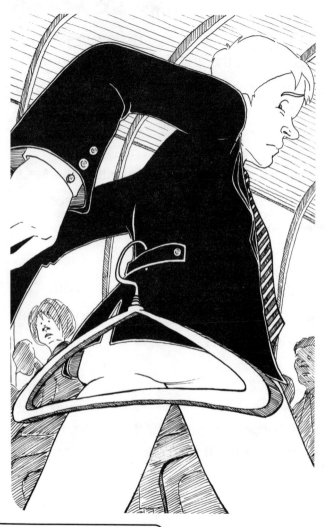

A Hanger On

What's in A Name

One of the stranger phone calls received at a dress shop was when a man identified himself as "Mr. Dress" and wanted to know if his wife was still there. The clerk, thinking that it was a crank call, hung up on him. He called back again and again, and received the same treatment. He finally called back and explained that it was not a crank call, that his wife was at the store, and that it was imperative that he speak to her. The clerk called out for Mrs. Dress, explaining that there was a call for her. There was actually a woman named Mrs. Dress in the store. The clerk will never forget that awkward moment!

Payroll Blues

While you are sitting around the table in the employee lounge with your co-workers, you bring up the hourly pay rates. You've just been transferred to this department and thought you would be paid a higher rate than you had received. After announcing your dissatisfaction to the others, they act shocked. Come to find out, you are making five dollars more an hour than any of them!

AWKWARD MOMENTS

The eager boat salesman repeatedly suggests to an interested buyer that he bring his wife into the showroom to show her the boat. He points out all the features women tend to appreciate.

Finally, the prospective buyer turns to the salesman and says, "I don't have a wife, I have a partner. And HE will come in tomorrow!"

Recalling a romantic event to friends, at a social gathering, thinking full well it was your spouse who shared this bit of history with you, then realizing halfway through the story that it was, in fact, an old flame.

Wearing shoes with black rubber soles and the head of maintenance tracks you down, because of the scuffmarks you are leaving everywhere.

More Famous Moments

Hugh Grant - Tonight Show appearance after encounter with a prostitute!

Marv Albert - Letterman appearance after having details revealed of how he dresses in a teddy!

David Letterman's interview with Drew Barrymore: she stood in front of him, and flashed him her breasts

Jim Baker's Scandal

Jimmy Swaggart's Scandal

A message from your Wife

All Sewn Up

A male bank president arrived one morning, disgruntled because a button had fallen off his suit coat on the way into work. Thinking nothing of it, he handed his coat to his secretary and asked that she sew the button on before his midmorning meeting. Wanting to be helpful, yet guarding against being taken advantage of, she sets to work. The bank president was pleased to find his button sewn on, but imagine his surprise when he realized that the newly replaced button kept his suit coat sewn shut! He laughed hardily, taking note that sewing buttons was never included in her job description.

The Invitation

Assuming that everyone in the office has been invited to the boss' daughter's baby shower, I asked during lunchtime, "I'm bringing a fruit salad to Mary Lou's party Friday night. Is anyone else bringing a dish?"

They all reply, "We weren't invited to any party!"

A Woman with a Reputation

My widowed mother was in her mid-seventies when she was "keeping company" with a gentleman. He spent one night at her apartment because he was too tired to drive home. I received a frantic phone call at 6:00 AM the following morning from Mom, asking for help, because she thought Mack was dead!

I guess I wasn't the only one she had called, because when I reached her apartment building, both the police and fire departments were already there. All of the neighbors were awake, looking out their windows, and watching as I arrived. They assumed that my mother had died-not the gentleman with whom she had been "keeping company". As I got to her apartment door, the EMT was pulling the sheet over Mack's head, indicating he had passed away.

Both my mother and I shared many awkward moments, not only when the neighbors saw mother alive and well, but now my poor mother was a woman with a "reputation"!

More than We Bargained For

It was the last few days of my junior year in college. Two of us were left in our apartment with little food, and no money. We had one exam to go and then we would leave the next day. But the problem was, we were starving! It was about 6:00 PM when we realized we had nothing to eat in the apartment. Going out to eat was out of the question, because we didn't have enough money, and yes, this was before MasterCard and Visa were created.

We emptied out our piggy banks, then checked the couches for loose change. We came up with $1.32. It was enough for a couple of boxes of macaroni and cheese mix. Jerry, my roommate, and I went to the supermarket. He wandered off, as I got the macaroni and cheese.

I even kidded him as he looked at the meat section, saying, "What are you dreaming?"

We went to check out, ready to pay with our pennies. The cashier got annoyed with us, because we were literally paying with pennies and a few nickels.

She disgustingly turned to me and asked, "What are you a couple of cheapskates?"

I was insulted with her tone of voice.

At that point, I was furious. I demanded to see the manager. Jerry, who was quiet up until this time, said, "Yes, we are, no big deal. We always act like this, and we are so sorry for any harm we have caused."

I turned to him and said, "What's wrong with you?"

He then said, "Stop it and leave this poor gal to do her job."

I didn't know what to say, so I just dropped it and left the store confused.

When we got to the car, Jerry pulled out a three pound T-bone steak which he had stuffed in the front of his white jeans. The meat that he had stolen was starting to leak. I could have killed him, but I wasn't about to go back to the store to return it, either. As a matter of fact, I never went in that store again. It was just too awkward.

Haste Makes Waste

After a long day in New York, my mother was rushing to catch the Boston shuttle. After she settled into her seat, the plane took off and she heard the pilot announce the weather conditions in Washington, DC. She immediately called the flight attendant and asked what the weather was in Boston. The flight attendant said she would find out. A moment later, she returned and reported the information to my mother.

The next announcement my mother heard was that they were approaching Washington, DC. Then panicked, she called the flight attendant again and asked why they were landing in Washington. After being told that this was a scheduled flight to Washington, D.C., they realized she had gotten on the wrong plane!

Educating Mom

Mom announced at dinner that she had seen a talk show that afternoon which was discussing sexual issues.

"I was wondering", she continued, "What's oral sex?"

My brother and sister-in-law sat stunned, too shocked to speak. As my Dad cleared his throat, I suggested to my older brother, "Paul, you tell her. You've known her longer!"

AWKWARD MOMENTS

Not having enough money, when checking out of a grocery store

Bumping a fellow shopper with your cart

Causing the grocery store display of cans to fall

Choosing the best-looking tomatoes, while causing the pile to cascade to the floor

Being caught sampling the fruit

If she only knew

Static Cling

The Turkey with A Secret

When I was eight years old, our Thanksgiving dinner was exceptionally special because we had extra relatives visiting. My parents got up early to get the turkey in the oven. It barely fit because the bird was so large.

We were awaiting the arrival of the turkey to grace the table, where my father would carve it just as in the classic Norman Rockwell painting. It seemed like we were waiting quite a while. So, being an impatient little boy, I decided to go into the kitchen and check things out. Just as I walked in, I saw my mother and father struggling to get the turkey out of the oven. My mother finally gave it a yank, and lo and behold, the turkey popped out of the oven and dropped on the floor into hundreds of little pieces! Suddenly, I felt my father's big hand cup my face.

He whispered into my ear, "Don't say one word about this, or you'll be grounded for the rest of my life."

I was told to say my father decided to carve the turkey in the kitchen this year. I did. Then I sat quietly and never mentioned it again. We weren't even allowed to joke about it until I graduated from college. That was the awkward moment that never went away.

AWKWARD MOMENTS

When you arrive late for your seminar on Time Management

When you send a demo tape to a talent agent, and you realize you've sent the wrong tape

When you proudly blurt out, "Here's that book!" while shuffling through your briefcase during your seminar on organization

When you send a demo tape to a talent agent and it doesn't work

When someone introduces you before a seminar and says the wrong name

How to Change Soiled to Sold

A friend of mine owns a downtown woman's apparel store where they were holding their Annual Old Fashioned Summer Sidewalk Sale. This is a sale where most of the merchandise is placed outside on racks in front of the store, at a greatly reduced price.   As the story goes, my friend was trying to decide whether or not to mark down a specific rack of dresses when he noticed a dog walking down the street.

As he thought to himself, "What a cute dog!" the dog stopped in front of the rack of dresses, lifted its leg, and relieved itself on the marked down merchandise. The worst part about the whole thing was that it happened in front of a sidewalk full of customers.

The moment was awkward until a customer broke the tension by asking, "How much more will those dresses be marked down?"

My friend thought fast and replied, "An additional 50% off."

The dresses were completely sold out in twenty minutes. The situation wasn't only awkward because of the dog peeing, but also because he had to put the wet sold dresses in the bags!

AWKWARD MOMENTS

When you arrive early to a seminar, question another early arrival about the effectiveness of the speaker, and you are actually talking to the speaker

When you are the guest speaker and the audience is introduced to a topic other than what you have prepared

When you forget the name of the group to whom you are speaking

When your microphone repeatedly cuts out on you while you are presenting a seminar

Hat Head

Squirting Lobster

When you fax a personal note to the wrong person

When you repeatedly fax to a person's telephone number

Credit card declined

When you make a mental note to clean out your car after work, and then your boss asks you to drive the office workers to the luncheon meeting

When you lie, saying you read the email they sent you, then getting caught in the lie

The Love Shop

When Rick was speaking at an annual meeting for the merchants at a mall in Texas, he was introduced to one merchant he will never forget. It was customary for him to introduce himself to as many people in the audience as possible. On this particular day, when introducing himself, he asked the merchant for the name of his store. Rick was then taken back when the merchant replied that it was the "Love Shop". His first thought was that the store sold "adult" toys, although it did seem a little strange to have that type of store in a first class mall.

But Rick, trying to be as flexible as possible, replied, "Hey, that must be a lot of fun working in a place like that!"

The merchant replied, "It's not what you think".

Rick replied, in a more suggestive manner, "It must be better!"

One more time, the merchant said that it wasn't what you think, until Rick finally asked "What is it, then?"

The merchant replied as innocently as possible, "It's a Christian Book Store".

At that point, Rick wanted to crawl under the counter.

When you can't remember your client's name while you are introducing him

When you've forgotten whether you pre-ordered fish or chicken while attending the office's banquet

When you send out two contracts to new clients, but you reverse the envelopes - and one is at a discount

When you're trying to make a good impression and you have an enormous run in your stockings

AWKWARD MOMENTS

When you burn a hole in your girlfriend's living room sofa

When you are caught by the police "parking" in the backseat, and you are helping your girlfriend put her clothes back on

When you try to act cool

When you can't remember your date's name

When you are with a friend, while she is kissing her boyfriend good-bye

The Interview

You have a two o'clock appointment with a prospective client, Mr. Doolittle, the CEO of a major corporation, who is extremely busy. He has agreed to see you, as a favor to a mutual friend. It's two o'clock and you are buzzing around the parking lot, desperate to find parking! Finally, in another aisle, you spot a car backing out, which sends you flying around to land on that spot. As you zoom in, another driver who was waiting for the leaving car to move, nearly hits your car. Total frustration consumes you as you yell out your window, "Hey Moron! Watch where you're going!"

You jump out of your car and slam the door. You frown and wave your hand again at the man behind the wheel, who sits watching you in total amazement of your bullish behavior. You make a mad dash to the office building. Out of breath and disheveled, you reach his office. His receptionist tells you that he has not yet returned from lunch, and to have a seat. Thankful to have a few minutes to pull yourself together, you retreat to a nearby chair.

Ten minutes later, the receptionist receives a call from her boss. He is ready for your appointment, so she directs you to his office door. Calmly, you prepare to enter his office, ready with your friendliest smile, to greet the man behind the door. How awkward you feel when you find that the moron in the parking lot is Mr. Doolittle!

THE END

More Awkward Moments to Come

As you have seen from reading this book (and undoubtedly experienced in your own life), awkward moments happen when we are least prepared. Which means that awkward moments happen everywhere; at work or home, with family, friends or strangers. This book tells of a variety of situations, involving a wide range of people. In collecting these stories, we realized that awkward moments are connected to every walk of life and to every stage of life, as a child, teenager, adult and senior citizen.

Therefore, this is the first of our series titled, "Awkward Moments: Celebrating the Humor in Life's Uncomfortable Situations". Our following publications will zero in on particular professions, careers, social events, family happenings, age groups and sexes. After reading our book, if you have an awkward moment you would like to share, logon to **www.AwkwardMoments.com** to submit your stories. In the meantime, remember compassion and well-meaning humor will lighten the burden of those unexpected awkward moments.

The Other Side of Wayne Gignac
How to contact him

Wayne Gignac, a *Humor Resources Specialist*, holds State of Connecticut teaching credentials and a degree in communications. Wayne works with companies, who want their employees to work better together, and with people, who want to enjoy what they do. An accomplished magician and standup comedian, Wayne weaves magic and humor to motivate, energize and communicate to his audiences, the importance of having fun at work, how to handle stress, and finding a balance between work and home. As director of The Show Works, Wayne has performed his unique training for many organizations, including the United States Postal Service, The American Bankers Association, McDonald's franchise owners, and thousands of bankers, in hundreds of banks all across the country. Thousands of Foxwood Casino employees have been trained to use Wayne's *Taking Care of You* approach, to customer service.

Wayne and Laura are in the process of completing *"I Can't Wait to Go to Work!"* a book based on the highly popular educational system that Wayne developed and delivered to audiences during the past decade. Wayne and Laura will be directing the Awkward Moments gang in the production of the next in the Awkward Moments series —*Awkward Moments in the Hospital* and *Awkward Moments in the Workplace*, both due out in 2002.

For more info or to send your stories, contact Wayne or Laura at:
Website: www.TheShowWorks.com
Email: Wayne@TheShowWorks.com
Phone: 860-887-7054
Fax: 860-892-1951
Pony Express: 30 Slater Avenue, Norwich, CT 06360

The Other Side of Rick Segel
How to contact him

Although Rick is known for his humor and quick wit he is also an international retailing expert. He conducts workshops, seminars, and after dinner talks with subjects ranging from humor as a tool in business, to economic forecasts for independent retailers, to how to make money in small business today. Everything that Rick does is always punctuated with his legendary side order of humor, fun, and his "laugh and learn" approach to business and life.

Rick is a Certified Speaking Professional (CSP) with over 1200 professional presentations. He is a past President of the National Speakers Association Chapter in New England and has authored *Laugh and Get Rich*, which has been translated into 3 different languages, and the best selling instructional retail book today, *Retail Business Kit for Dummies*, published by Hungry Minds.

To get in touch with Rick, try one of the following means:

Web Address www.ricksegel.com
Email: rick@ricksegel.com
Phone: 781-272-9995
Fax: 781-272-9996
Snail mail: 1 Wheatland Street, Burlington, MA 01803

Specific House Publishing
Quick Order Form

Awkward Moments
Celebrating The Humor in Life's Uncomfortable Situations

 Fax orders: (781) 272-9996

 Phone orders: (781) 272-9995
Please have your credit card ready

 Postal orders: Specific House Publishing,
One Wheatland St., Burlington, MA 01803

Please send me _____ copies of *Awkward Moments* at $11.95 each, plus shipping and handling.

Name: _____
Address: _____
City: _____ State: _____ Zip: _____
Phone: _____
Email address: _____

Sales tax: Please add 5% for products shipped to Massachusetts addresses.

Shipping: **US:** $4 for the first book and $2 for each additional book.
International: Based on ship-to location and current rates; please call for exact amounts.

Payment type: ❏ Check enclosed ❏ Credit card
❏ Visa   ❏ Mastercard   ❏ American Express

Credit card #: _____

Name on card: _____ exp date: _____ / _____